My Wills' Way

Dominique Cesar

My Wills' Way

By

Dominique Cesar

Illustrations by William L Cesar

Amazon Kindle Direct Publishing

www.kdp.amazon.com

References

"Frayed Wire" an article by Lori Sealy in *The Aquilla Report, 2016.*

"Why autistic kids make easy targets for school bullies" an article by Maia Szalavits in *Time Magazine, 2012.*

'Thanksgiving" The true story, a book written by Penny Colman, *2008.*

"Emmet Till: The Murder That shocked the World and Propelled the Civil Rights Movement", a book written by Devery S. Anderson, 2015.

"Cop shoots caretaker of autistic man playing in the streets with a toy" an article by Charles Rabin in *The Miami Herald, 2016.*

Dedicated to Randy Eugene Benjamin

This book is for my children and mother. To William and Christian I am blessed to have been chosen to be the one to bring into this world. Stay true to yourself. I am proud of you. Always remember that you are my sunshine and I love you. To my mother, thank you for being my best friend and Superhero when I needed one. You continue to believe in me. I am the woman I am today because of you; you are the best.

Table of Contents

Preface

I have often wondered if being a parent was hard. Like every other child, I was naive and believed that it was fun and seemed like one of the natural things a person can do. My perception of life was pure. My priorities were doing what I enjoyed. I played with my toys and spent time with my friends and family. My mother and I were close. I was her little princess, and she was my best friend. My mother was a great foundation and inspiration. She made it look effortless. Her attitude was always so vibrant and upbeat, assuring a childhood filled with love and joy. Left with beautiful memories,

It did not occur to me until I would have children of my own, motherhoods no piece of cake. Like me, my mother would spoil my children, as well. To be honest, I could not complain. My children were blessed to have everything that their hearts desired. Time after time, either my mother or stepfather would come home from work with a gift at hand. It was Christmas for them every day. I did not think it was necessary. I love to put a smile on their faces, but It did not warrant being broke. Within a couple of days, they would grow bored, lose, or destroy them. Fortunately, like clockwork, they would receive another one.

I tried speaking with my parents several times, but it seemed to fall on deaf ears. So, I stopped trying and accepted that there was no compromising when it came to their grandchildren. One late afternoon, my mother came home and presented a gift to my eldest son, William. "Hey!" she yelled. "After work, I decided to stop by a toy store to see if I can find anything that my beautiful grandson will like!" "After searching for a while, I found this book that has a small piano attached. It guides children to play". She said. Excited to see his reaction, she walked briskly to his room and retrieved him. Sitting him down on the dining room chair, she placed the book on his lap and waited patiently for a reaction.

I looked; it was a hardcover book for children. It had a different song on every page and instructions on how to play. Amazingly, he began to smile once he started to open the pages and playing with miniature keys. "what do u think?" she asked. "I think he'll enjoy playing with it," I said with a smirk and walked away as he continued to enjoy his new toy. We began to converse on how the day went. Amid her rambling about her daily gossip, she abruptly stops. As if she was in a trance, she slowly turns her head to me and asks. "Do you hear that? "Hear what"? I replied, perplexed. "That music, where is it coming from? I think it is coming from his new toy". I stopped for a second and listened for what captivated her attention. The music was delightful. It was classical and flowed beautifully. "The music that the toy comes with sounds nice," she says with a smile. I nodded, "yes, it does. I'm glad that you bought it for him." "me, too!" we agreed.

It was perfect, it seemed to keep him occupied, and he was enjoying himself. He began to giggle and laugh as I approached him. I noticed him playing the piano. What caught my attention was how he was playing with it. At that moment, I realized that the toy did not come with any preset music.it was all coming from him, and he was playing at three years old. His fingers placed as if he mastered it. It was the most incredible sight to behold, a piano savant, the sounds where not one of an amateur but a person who had the gift of music flowing so divinely in his veins.

"Mommy, come over here!" I yelled, calling her to the living room to see it for herself. As soon as she walked in and noticed it, her eyes lit up brighter than a lightbulb. She could not hold back her astonishment; she ran over to him and gave him a big hug. Sharing the same sentiment, I stood there in amazement and humbly gave him one as well. I held him in my arms, thanking my creator for blessing me with such a fantastic child. I promised him that I would do everything I could to help nurture his talents. Little did I know in that moment of excitement, neither of us could have predicted the rollercoaster of the journey.

Acknowledgments

I Appreciate the love and gratitude that I have received from my Friends and Family throughout the process of writing this book. Thank You for your support. To my love, I cherish and adore you always.

Chapter 1

Simple Beginnings

The Abandonment Cycle Begins

As far back as my earliest memory, my mother was a "Single Mom." At the age of 35, she was working as a secretary and living in New York City. She was independent and enjoyed traveling with her friends all over the world. She visited Africa, Gabon, Cameroon, Nigeria, Senegal, Ivory Coast. Paris, France, Amsterdam in the Netherlands, Italy, Greece, Switzerland, Brussels, Caracas, Venezuela, Mexico, Hawaii, Trinidad, Brazil. St Martin, St. Thomas, Barbados, and Aruba.

Although traveling seemed to have been her favorite hobby, her true love was children. My mother was and still is terrific with kids. She was the one that her friends would usually turn to for help with their children. Once she finally decided to have her own, she was unable to carry them to term and, unfortunately, suffered five miscarriages.

Under a lot of pressure, she decided to move back to Haiti for a while to recover. During that process, she met and fell in love with my father. They became good friends before they allowed their romance to bud. Once they did, she became pregnant. She was happy, anxious, scared, and cautious. She knew she wanted to be a mother, but she was afraid of facing disappointment again after trying and failing many times.

She stayed positive and had faith that she would soon have the family that she always wanted. Through her strength and perseverance, she carried on and gave birth to a healthy and beautiful baby girl. I was born in 1984 in Port-au-Prince, Haiti. The year Gandhi was assassinated, the AIDS virus identified, and the MTV Music Awards began. Movie Classics such as Ghostbusters, Police Academy, and Terms of Endearment were released. It was the year that launched Miami Vice and the Introduction of crack cocaine to the black community. A gallon of gas cost $1.10, and a movie ticket was $2.50. It was (in my opinion) the best era to have grown up. The Hip Hop culture was reaching its pinnacle of influence as it reached the masses.

Shortly after giving birth to me, it all collapsed. Unfortunately, my parents' relationship ended when my mother found out that my father was cheating and had another family with another woman. I was too young to be aware of what was transpiring. I spent a lot of time alone. To make up for the lack of siblings, I stayed in the company of friends and family. I felt lucky to have spent the beginning of my life encompassed by people who had my best interest at heart.

Our family lived on a vast sprawl of land my great grandfather owned. He was a well-known businessman from a mountainous region called Delmas. My mother had two older siblings, a brother and sister. By the time I was born, my Aunt had given birth to 10 children, sadly, not all survived. A couple of years after my uncle died. My Aunt's children were in their mid and late 20' s and had started families of their own. Therefore, since they were already adults, I grew up with their children, my second cousins.

My mother went back to the United States. Once my residency settled, she and I settled in Queens Village, New York. We stayed for one year. She was laid off and no longer worked in the same profession. She decided to change paths and work for a bank. Part of the transition was that we had to move back to Haiti.

We moved in with one of my mother's nieces and her husband (who was also my Godfather). They had two daughters Tamie and Ariel. At the same time, My Mother's favorite niece and her daughter (another second cousin) Jojo, decided to move from New York as well. To my surprise, Jojo and I bonded better than with the others. We shared the same personality traits and loved the same things. We sang aloud our favorite songs, watched our favorite TV shows.

We became the best of friends. We Played with toys and shared secrets only with each other. Sadly, after six months, Jojo and her Mother moved back to Brooklyn. When she left, I felt like I lost my best friend. As time went on, the rift I was feeling amongst the others grew. Once, I considered them my sisters, but I noticed changes that were not subtle. I was acknowledging a bit more, precisely the nature of my environment. It was just ...awful.

The Harsh Reality

As children, we wear our "Veils of Innocence "until we undergo many of life's unpleasantries. Once ripped off, part of processing changes is by acknowledging the need for it. I was already aware that the people that I was living with (although they were my family) were different. In terms of color and classism, their social status was different than others. At the age of five, I enrolled in" La Petite Sirene," the best Montessori school in the region. I loved to dance, especially Ballet, so my mother allowed me to take lessons. By all accounts, I was doing what I love, having a wonderful childhood.

Unfortunately, I noticed that the other children around me were growing up in poverty. My veil did not allow me to understand, nor could I fathom that we were living in the most impoverished country in the Western Hemisphere. Except for a few, most of our neighbors lived in make-shift shack houses. People lived off whatever they could sell growing from the land or anything that their creativity could produce. Both adults and children would beg as a means of survival. The people who could afford to live comfortably did so by employing live-in servants. My Godfather was one of them. He was the manager of an affluent hotel in Port-au-Prince. He provided for his family very well, so much so that his wife (my cousin) could afford not to work and solely depend on their live-in servant.

The social construct usually determined who would make a sufficient servant. 10 out of 10, it would be someone who shared my dark skin complexion. Historically, fairer skin was associated with wealthy people because it meant that they did not have to labor in the sun all day. The conflict (for me) is that it is customary for the children of the servants to follow in their parents' footsteps and become the next generation of maids. I observed how social hierarchy worked, and I was not impressed. It shaped how I viewed my own family. My Mother and I were (still are) the darkest ones in the immediate family. I felt like the literal "Black Sheep." At times I felt like an "ugly duckling." Despite being amongst other children (After my favorite cousin left), I found myself yearning for the companionship of someone I felt would be close to me enough to completely understand and not judge like a biological sibling or even my mom. Because of the nature of her job, she was busy traveling while I was tearing the veil to shreds.

I was always shunned and made to feel like I was the "Black Sheep" of the family. I secluded myself because I did not feel like I had anything in common with them, and I was not relevant.

They always had an air of bourgeoisie to them. Some were continually striving to be part of the upper echelon. They kept tripping over their egos. The saying is, "Money doesn't buy class"! They lived comfortably but were treating others around them poorly. They were looking down on people who were not as fortunate. They were not the only offenders to this type of prejudice. I saw many others (fair skin) individuals with the same "God amongst men" superiority complex. It is an attitude that is prevalent across the country. Instead of camaraderie, they settle with hierarchy.

The idea of being charitable was not an aspect of their lives. I came across many people who were either middle class or poor and in constant survival mode. I was fortunate to be acquainted with truly kind people. They did not have much as far as possessions. They were selfless, thinking of others and not just for themselves. I related more to them and began to detest people that behaved like the ones in my family.

Colorism

"Colorism" is the practice of discrimination by which those with lighter skin are treated more favorably than those with darker skin. This practice is a product of racism in the United States. It upholds the White Anglo-Saxon standards of beauty and benefits the institutions of oppression (Politics, media, etc.)."

It is evidence of the indelible marks of slavery. It has been both psychological and social hindrance to our progress. The idea that "White" and "Light" are right and "Black and "Brown" is wrong. Perpetuated during slavery, subconsciously embedded in the minds of those who deal with the lack of self-love, social and economic disparities. Darker-skinned individuals like myself had to learn to navigate my true feelings due to the respect that we have for our elders. I felt a mixture of confusion, sorrow, and hate.

It broke my heart to see others going through immense social and economic oppression. Some members of my own family treated me less than kind. Seldomly was I complimented or acknowledged by them when I felt beautiful in a new dress or mastered a new move I learned in Ballet. Unlike me, they gave their children the approval and praise they sought.

Their eyes lit up as their children and others that looked similar said or did something worthy of their praise. At times, the children would refuse to play with me. The adults would use me as a pawn in an argument about who is the child was better by comparison. Finally, they would give me the things that they did not want themselves or their children, i.e., food, toys, clothes.

The living conditions were dire. To make it worse, we were discriminating against our people. I was treated differently and wondered if it was because I was the "Black Sheep." Others believed so due to my juvenile mistakes. At one point, I began to think that I was just inherently "Evil." After the "veil" slowly tore away and disintegrated, I was finally able to see people for who they indeed were. I learned early to accept people for who they are and not to let them affect the glow of my outer and inner beauty.

Chapter 2

<u>Flying Above It All</u>

New Horizons

Despite the disappointing aspects of my environment, I enjoyed my childhood. My mother was terribly busy and tried her best to raise me. After a while of working abroad, the distance began to take its toll. My mother and I traveled back and forth between New York and Haiti, so she opted to find another job. We decided that it was an opportune time to leave the country.

The prospects of moving back to the United States was exciting. My native language was French, but I understood English. We went to Miami, Florida, in the spring of 1993. We resided in a one-bedroom Duplex in the Suburbs. It was small, beautiful, and quiet. My school was only one block away, but the transition was not smooth. I was anxious, anticipating making friends and starting a new chapter. Before our arrival, a category five hurricane made landfall in the Southeastern United States. We resided in an area that was not profoundly affected. Still recovering from the damages suffered from Hurricane Andrew, moving to Florida at that time was not easy.

When we left Haiti, I was in the middle of my second-grade school year. Besides acclimating to my new environment, part of the requirements for my International transfer was to take a test to assess my competency level. To all our surprise, I scored above average within the United States Education Systems Standards and immediately promoted to the fourth grade.

It was both exciting and challenging. I decided that whatever the experience would be that I would be happy that I would be able to be with my mother. She instilled her views of life in me, and I used it to make her proud of me. She encouraged me to be a Leader and not a Follower. Goodness knows I needed that advice. Being so young, I gravitated towards the older, accessible, not so lovely kids. To "buy" friends, I got in trouble several times. My mother decided that I needed to work on my self-confidence.

My first year in the American educational system was challenging because of the language barrier. I attended Williams Jennings Bryant Elementary school. First, I had to learn the language. My mother arranged for my fourth-grade teacher (who was kind enough) to tutor me after school. She came to my house three to four days a week to teach me how to speak English. Thanks to her help, I was able to assimilate.

I enjoyed reading, writing, and learning. I always tried my best Throughout elementary and middle school and earned straight A's. I dealt with being bullied and ostracized because I was considered one of the "smart kids." Often, I was teased and called a "Teacher's pet," "Nerd," and "Frog Eyes."

At the time, I did not understand why people were so mean to me. Granted, I did have to wear prescription glasses, and they were Steve Urkel inspired Coke bottle glasses. I just did not feel that it warranted all the hatred that came my way. My mother would always just tell me that the other kids were just jealous of me. She was still supportive and nurtured my talents. With her encouragement, I Kept my integrity and continued to strive for my Academic achievements. I overcame it all and even led my class by having the highest grades and best attitude towards my favorite thing in the world Learning!

It took me a while to understand that not everyone appreciated and loved learning as I did. One thing I loved to learn was dancing. I continued to pursue it. I enrolled in dance classes at the "Turning Point Dance Academy." For eight years, classically trained in Ballet, Jazz, Tap, Flamenco, African, Contemporary, Irish-Step, and Hip Hop. The art of Dance helped me to express myself and "break out of my shell," so to speak. I developed my confidence and learned to value my talents and myself.

My Dance instructor Mrs. Skeele believed in Philanthropy, so we did several performances as part of our community service initiative. Such as Nursing Homes, County Fairs, Libraries, and even movie sets such as "Any Given Sunday," Starring Jamie Foxx, Dennis Quaid, and Camron Diaz. I earned several awards throughout the years, including a Dance scholarship.

One of the most significant opportunities presented to me was joining a magnet program and attending the best high school in Miami. I applied and was one of only two students accepted from the middle school I attended. It was about an hour and a half away from where I lived. I was thirteen years old and a freshman. It was challenging. I was used to being the smartest fish in the pond now. I had to cope with being a young, small fish in a big sea surrounded by "Older" fish.

It did not take a long time to figure out that the "Magnet" program was a group of selected kids bused from the inner city to an affluent area to attend a "prestigious" school — located in a predominantly Hispanic neighborhood. Throughout high school, I did not attempt to make friends or include my peers. I focused on school.

Freshman year, I did not know anyone and did not feel like anyone wanted to know me. It might have been all in my head, but I was an Introvert I dealt with everything internally. I was a bit more concerned with my studies. Eventually, I did try to "branch out" to encompass everything that was the "High school" experience. My Sophomore year was when I decided to join Track and Field and the schools' Dance Troupe. I wanted to be part of the experience. Like any typical high school setting, different social groups founded by individual interests. Now I was tasked to find where I belonged.

On top of the pyramid were "The Jocks," which consisted of Athletes and Cheerleaders. The other, less popular layers were the "Rich" kids, The "Band Kids', the "Nerds," etc. I hung out with the socially awkward group, better known as the "Goth "kids. They were the Anarchist, non-conforming, socialist outcasts that I identified. I hung around them because I did not feel judged, I could be myself, and no matter how "Weird" someone might think I was, deep down I knew I was part of a clan that was just like me. I was not alone anymore.

Throughout high school, I joined many extra-curricular activities. I took part in the Debate team. Junior Year, I created my dance troupe and named it "The Nubian Queens." Between taking dance lessons and having my own Dance Troupe, I somehow found time always to stay involved in community service.

I spent my summer breaks attending summer school. I did not like to stay at home. I elected to go because I wanted to not because I had to. I did so until the school's administration decided I could not take "Extra" Credit Courses anymore.

Due to my hectic schedule, High School was a busy time for me. I did not notice that my peers had been paying attention to me. Towards the end of my Senior year of high school, we had to vote for "Class Superlatives." To my surprise, they nominated me for "Friendliest," "Most Athletic," and "Most Talented." I did not win any of the categories, but the fact that I was acknowledged made me feel special. All I had to do was be me.

Spreading My Wings

I began high school at thirteen years old and graduated at the age of 16, the youngest graduate from my class. The most pivotal point of my life was also the most confusing. I wanted to join the armed forces but was too young. I decided that because I was so young, it was best that I stayed home for a while. Two weeks later, I began the Summer semester at Miami Dade College. I honestly did not have a clear goal for myself nor my life. I was extremely young for everything I was experiencing. I knew that I was gifted academically, but socially I was an immature and indecisive teenager.

Once I began to attend college, after a semester, I started having trouble at home with my stepfather. I always kept my relationship with him at bay. We never became close; we were still cordial for my mother's sake. The relentless arguing was too overwhelming, and I felt the need to leave home finally. I was 17 when I transferred to Bethune Cookman College in Daytona Beach, Florida. The prospects of the decision seemed promising. It was only four hours from home, and It was a private school with excellent credentials. As excited as I was to continue my education in such an extraordinary institution, I was dependent on financial Aide, and the school had been receiving limited funding, so eventually, I came across financial hardships.

Be All that I can Be

After three semesters, I was struggling to stay in school. Despite trying to secure employment, my age kept me at a disadvantage. I could barely afford to eat. I became depressed, and my attitude changed. I began making reckless decisions. I got into some trouble and had to deal with the consequences. Feeling overwhelmed, I decided that it was best that I came back home and continued my education.

Transitioning from a teenager into adulthood was not an easy process (especially decision making). I felt like a failure when I came back home. My depression did not seem to go away. At some point, I felt like I was going in the wrong direction. I had not pinpointed a career yet nor what my life plan. After having a long talk with my mother, she felt that my problem was that I lacked discipline and no structure. In high school, I wanted to join the United States Air Force. I graduated from school at an early age. Therefore, I was too young to join the military. Now that I was about to turn 19, I considered it again. I concluded that joining the military was the best avenue for me to get back on the road to fulfillment.

In 2002, President George W. Bush declared war on Iraq I joined ten months later. I opted to enter the United States Navy because of the chance to be on the water, to travel, and expand my horizons. I knew that there was a significant chance that I would end up in combat. When I finalized my decision, I left for Great Lakes, Illinois. There I attended "Boot Camp" and trade school. The training was twelve weeks of intense, grueling workouts and psychological breakdowns. I was pushed to the limit physically and mentally. I tried my best and kept pushing myself, no matter what. In the end, I surpassed my expectations.

Chosen to be first in command for my division, which consisted of 27 men and 12 women, I was the youngest. The oldest in our ranks was 35 years old. I was a 19-year-old When I entered Boot Camp. A 5" 5, 155-pound girl in charge of a group of Alpha, Competitive, testosterone-driven males. When I first began handing down their orders, they were reluctant to listen. Then they began to become defiant and disrespectful. After brooding for a couple of days, I concluded that I had to make my presence known and demand respect. I had to utilize my leadership skills and become more confident in who I was. I began asserting my authority and making sure with the understanding that It was part of my job. I was able to move forward without incident. I commanded the respect that I deserved and did my work to the best of my ability.

I went to boot camp for three months. After Boot Camp, we had to endure an additional and three weeks of Trade school. When Trade School was over, I could go home for a week before leaving for duty—stationed in Norfolk, Virginia, on board the DDG 87 USS Mason.

I excelled in my military career. I was promoted three times within the first two months of enlisting. I was proficient at most of the tasks assigned to me. I pulled lines and helped anchor ships. Jobs that required a minimum of four people I was to do alone, I enjoyed life at sea. The companionship between my shipmates and I made the experience bearable. We traveled to many places, such as Hawaii, California, and Japan. As time went on, I started to succumb to the environment. The small, coffin-shaped beds in the small confined barracks that we all had to share became my nightmare. I found myself breathing heavily and uneasy. I discovered that I am claustrophobic and was experiencing anxiety attacks. Slowly but surely it was becoming clear that It was not the life for me.

I confided my troubles to my Commanding Officer shortly before our ship was to be deployed to Afghanistan. I had to consult with a Psychiatrist and referred to Shore duty on the base. After a lengthy and arduous process. I received an "Honorable Discharge" from the military due to "Mental Health" Issues. Still depressed and feeling defeated, the daunting realization set in. I had to return home a failure AGAIN.

Once I was back home, I became a withdrawn pessimist. My outlook was bleak and gray. I hit rock bottom. I finally decided to seek professional help. It took me a long time to recover. I felt like a complete and utter loser. Until that point in my life, I considered myself somewhat of an overachiever. I fell hard from grace and stayed down for a long time. After taking the opportunity to reflect on what I wanted for myself, I learned to stop beating myself up for the past and focus on being the best version of myself for the future. I had to move forward with both life and love.

Chapter 3

<u>Abandoned and Pregnant</u>

Someone New

The process of self-evaluation is complicated. Once I was able to pinpoint where I was going wrong. I reevaluated my priorities and set some life goals. I researched and found a Vocational program to become a Pharmacy Technician. I wanted to attend school and gain a career path that would allow me to be independent. Nowhere in my plans did I anticipate meeting someone.

One day while I was running errands, upon entering the market, I came across an old friend Andy. He and I knew each other from middle school. Accompanied by someone I did not recognize. To my surprise, he did remember me after so long. I am glad because it would have been extremely awkward if he had not because I could not keep myself from staring. We caught a glimpse of each other and finally acknowledged each other. After catching up with the responses of the usual questions,

"Hey!" "How are you?" "How Have you been?" and "What have you been up to?". After giving short responses such as..." I'm fine," "you know the same old, same old." Or the best one, "You know just trying to survive another day (Insert fake laugh) ...you know?!"

My interest did not surpass a "Hi" and "Bye," but he insisted on conversing and decided to introduce me to his friend Winston. He was accompanying him during his tasks.

I take it he did not want him to feel left out. For some reason, the conversation directed towards inquiring about my love life. "Are you single?" he asked. I smiled and nodded. When he had the answer, he sought he somehow felt obliged to cure me of my "Single Woman Syndrome" by playing matchmaker.

To be frank, the only thing that I did learn about him that day was that he recently moved back to Miami from Chicago. Honestly, I was too tired to care. At that point, I was running late for work. After some small talk, I turned to him and said not to give him my number because he was a stranger to me. We walked away knowing that it would be inevitable that we would meet again, we did.

We crossed each other's path several times before I decided I wanted to know more about him and finally exchanged numbers. He seemed genuinely nice and charming, and it was a whirlwind romance. Everything seemed to happen so quickly. I was not thinking that I was meeting my future husband. I thought that I might have found someone to confide and befriend.

Unexpected

Winston and I began dating a couple of months after our first introduction. It turns out that we had many similar attributes and hobbies in common. We shared the same interests and spent most of our time together. Our time spent frequently going to dinner, movies, sporting events, and just taking random strolls in the park. Our relationship became an escape from the prior disappointments that I experienced. To fate's amusement and our surprise, we became closer with the help of a natural disaster.

In October 2005, Hurricane Wilma ravaged the state of Florida. The aftermath was horrible. The damage from the fallen trees and power lines with debris was horrific. Millions of people spent several weeks without electricity. The city had to comply with a mandatory curfew. Everyone had to be in their homes from Dusk until Dawn. Those who got caught after dark were ticketed for the violation or spend the night in jail. One evening,

Winston got captured by the Police Officer walking around his neighborhood after curfew. He received a ticket and fined because he was intoxicated and held overnight. The next day, after being released from the county jail, I went to visit him, I was worried. We sat and started commiserating over what transpired the night before. He explained, "I was grieving the loss of my uncle. I had just found out that he had passed that morning. I cried for a while and wanted to calm down, so I drank a couple of shots of alcohol.

I wanted some fresh air, so I left my house to take a walk". He continued, "The Police Officer spotted me a block from my house. I explained to him that m house was right there. I left my wallet at home, so he did not believe me. He gave me a ticket for being out past curfew and told me I was also under arrest for Public Intoxication." I felt terrible for him, so I decided to spend the night. We sat, had some wine, and spoke for hours. By the time, the sun had rose, the combination of anger from his ordeal, boredom, and alcohol, Ignited the passion, and we found comfort in each other's arms. My son conceived on that night.

It took a long time for everything to get back to normal. I went back to a daily routine, not thinking very much of that night. For three months, everything seemed okay until I missed my menstrual cycle. I quickly took a pregnancy test, and once It was confirmed, I was in a state of shock. I was Pregnant!!

My Previous health diagnosis revealed that it would be difficult to carry a child to full term with no complications due to the cysts on my ovaries. Although I was excited, I decided not to tell my parents. I felt I could wait to break the news to my mom until he and I spoke and completely understood the magnitude of the responsibilities that we were about to embark. Just me being naive with my decision making again.

When I told Winston, his initial reaction to the news was happiness. He was delighted and excited about the prospect of becoming a father. It was a first for both of us, and we wanted to be the best parents to our child. He also decided that he would only share the news with a limited number of friends and family. I was 22 years old and no longer a child. I also was not married and working part-time while attending school. I was nervous and scared. I wanted my prospect to consist of a direction and a level of control. I had created a path for myself that I had to derail now. Not being married and having a child out of wedlock was an issue for me. I somehow made myself believe that it was unacceptable. I thought that my mother and others would look down on me. I was ashamed.

I felt overwhelmed and needed time to figure out how I was going to break the big news to everyone. It was then that I decided that it would be best to hide my pregnancy. It made sense to me at the time. I naively believed that if I had the support of my child's father, it was all that I needed.

Abandoned

We were not married, but he assured me that he would be the best father to our child that he could be. I scheduled my first doctor's appointment. The plan was he would accompany me. That morning, I called to confirm that he woke up and would be ready to go on time. To my dismay, he did not answer any of my phone calls or texts, that day, nor the next.

I was not able to contact either him or his friends or family for over two weeks. My first reaction to the situation was to worry. I did not know his whereabouts. I thought something horrible could have happened to him. Finally, I was able to get in touch with his mother, who informed me that weeks earlier (the day of my doctor's appointment), he promptly left Miami for New York.

I was abandoned and ashamed for the choices that I made. I still did not dare to tell my parents about what I was going through. I fell into another state of depression. It was a one that I could not stay in for long. I dealt with anxiety, morning sickness, hormonal, and body changes without anyone suspecting a thing (so I thought). I was going to my monthly checkups and taking my prenatal vitamins. I am not sure if I thought it through entirely because I did not factor in that I would be going through noticeable physical changes. My body changing prompted questions and reason for the inquiry into my well-being.

My mother noticed that I was often sleeping, vomiting, and having constant mood swings, aside from the fact that I was getting massive. The curiosity was too much for her until she bluntly asked me once, "Are You Pregnant?". At that point, I felt that I had to honest. I was suffering in silence and needed someone. I knew deep inside the decision to withhold something so big from my mother was wrong. I was afraid of disappointing her AGAIN.

I finally confessed to her that yes, I was pregnant. Her reaction was a surprise. She was happy but disappointed that I took so long to come to her. Devasted, I did not feel like I could go to her with something so troubling. She said, "You Chose to suffer alone. You know that I will be there for you no matter what!". She hugged me and promised to be there for me from then on.

I was encouraged at the fact that I finally had the love and support that I needed. My 5-month checkup was significant because I was finding out the sex of my child. When I received a sonogram and a confirmation, it was a boy. To my surprise, both my mother and stepfather were incredibly supportive. They were not particularly pleased with the fact that the father of my child abandoned me. My mom was excited that she was about to become a grandmother.

She reassured me that I would not be going through it alone anymore, and I could always turn to my friends and family. It was then I decided that the nature of the relationship between his father and me meant nothing. I would be both father and mother to my child. I would shower him with all the love and attention that he would ever need. He would be the only man that truly mattered to me.

It was a bit surreal to realize that I would have my first child unmarried send alone. It was a hard time in my life. I would go through bouts of depression. I did not want to be a statistic. I wanted better for my son. I did not have the opportunity to grow up with my father. Although, I had a stepfather that came later in my life. In my subconscious mind, it was not an adequate replacement that I wanted. I was devastated at the prospect of having to raise a child alone. I was terrified that I would not make a good mother. At that point, I had not completed my degree; therefore, I knew I would endure financial hardship. Thankfully, I had supportive parents that made me see that the world and my future were not over. I would have just to work harder and stay determined to achieve my goals.

Chapter 4

A New Path

Having a Child

The remainder of my pregnancy was nothing but incredible. My due date was my birthday. It was the ultimate present that someone could ask. Leading up to the birth, I did everything that I was supposed to. I ate adequately, exercised, and took my prenatal vitamins daily. Despite doing everything that I could to prepare, there was still an underlying fear that I of being a good mother. After confiding in my mother, she suggested that I take parenting courses to help my confidence. I was referred to the local hospital and enrolled in "Parenting classes for New Expecting Mothers." I learned a lot of helpful information. I wanted to make sure that I would be a great mom and tried everything "by the book." I wanted to make sure that I was ready.

At eight months, I reluctantly held my baby shower. I still felt weird about being a single mother my first time around and having a child out of wedlock. It was small and intimate. Despite the constant feeling of loneliness and bouts of anxiety, that day felt like I was part of something bigger than myself. It was a small and intimate event with about 40 people, and I felt nothing but positive energy from everyone. I received plenty of gifts and well wishes. By then, I weighed over 200 pounds. With the birth drawing near (along with my size inflating), I grew more and more uncomfortable.

To entertain we, my mother and I would sit on a couch across from each other, watching the baby maneuver in my belly. We would guess the body part that he would be protruding. As mundane as it might have seemed, it was a great source of joy. When we were deciding on his name, we came up with almost 20 options but could not agree on one. Until we began discussing our "favorite people," and I suggested President Bill Clinton.

We looked at each other and thought that "William" seemed to fit very well. My mother helped tremendously and wanted to do something in honor of her. She was the youngest amongst her siblings and considered "Daddy's little girl." She loved her father very much. She told stories of being treated like a porcelain doll and always spoke highly of him. So, I wanted to name him after my grandfather Louis Cesar. Upon hearing this, she turned to me, smiled with great content, and agreed.

Although the baby was due on my birthday, he decided that he would come out on his own time. My delivery was scheduled a week after my due date. By then, I gained 75 pounds. The appointment was for Friday, August 18. In the early morning hours of Thursday, the 17th, I woke up thinking that I just needed to use the restroom. Instead, I placed my feet on the floor, and my water broke. Amidst the alarm and confusion, I began to scream for help. My mother heard my cries and helped me get cleaned up. I had already packed my bag, so I grabbed it, and we rushed to the hospital.

Upon our arrival, I was in much pain. I begged for anything to help me endure. The Anesthesiologist was not on duty. Therefore, I did not receive any pain killers. I was in labor for 16 hours when one finally was on duty. By the time she came in, I was clutching the guard rails on the hospital bed, begging someone to put me out of my misery. I breathed a sigh of relief when I finally received an epidural. For an additional 17 hours, I endured contractions every 6 minutes. Although I was doing my best, and he still was not making much progress. The Doctor then explained to me that the problem was the size of his head. It was larger than my cervix, and I needed an episiotomy. They needed to make an incision in the perineum to ensure he would have safe passage. After the procedure, he finally began to crown, the Doctor then informed and complimented me on his full curly hair head. She played with it. It was awkward. When his whole body finally came out, I breathed a sigh of relief. His eyes were wide open, and he was silent. I was worried, but instead of crying, he urinated all over the Doctor.

A Blessing

William Louis Cesar was born on August 18, 2006, at 7 pm. He weighed 7 pounds, 6 ounces. Being in labor for 33 hours affected my body tremendously. I had to undergo an episiotomy because his head was 13 cm. Due to pushing for so long, I developed a hernia. It would be an astute assessment to conclude that I was a "bit" naïve to what childbirth would be. It was the turning point in my life.

The hospital placed me in a recovery room by myself. After a couple of days, we were given a clean bill of health and allowed to go home. When I arrived, I received with huge "Welcome Home" and "Congrats" gestures from our family and friends. After everyone admired the baby and went home, I finally was able to get some rest. The first 24 hours of being home was a blur. I was exhausted, so I spent most of it asleep. I did not get much of a chance to get to any at the hospital.

The next morning after waking up to his cries of hunger and the need for a diaper change. I received an unexpected phone call from the hospital. They informed me that he had to take several tests during our stay, and the results drew concern. They were worried that he might have an infection. They advised me to admit him to the Miami Children's Hospital as soon as possible. They would have to administer additional tests to be able to conclude an accurate diagnosis.

I quickly packed his bags and informed my parents to meet us at the hospital. Within an hour, I had arrived. It would take a couple of days to determine what the problem was. For three days and two nights, I stayed by his side. They ran countless tests and finally concluded that the initial Culture Exam was contaminated, and he did not have any disorders. "Thank Goodness....," I told myself. As I stared gleefully into my healthy baby boy's eyes." Thank Goodness, he was completely healthy." After almost two days of labor and 72 hours of worry, I could finally draw a sigh of relief.

A New Mother

Being a first-time mother, I had a lot of preconceptions about what motherhood would be. I believe the word "naïve" can best describe my initial approach. Realistically, it was exhausting and painful. Despite how much I prepared for it, it was unpredictable. I wanted to make sure that I was the best mother I could be. It was a challenging beginning. Changing his diapers and feeding him every three hours. The crying, the pooping, spitting, and bathing was a lot to get used.

It was a period of adjustment. I intended to breastfeed for four months. It only lasted for two months until the exhaustion got to me, and I decided to give both formula and breastmilk. By the time William was five months old, I had given up pumping all together. I took him to all scheduled Doctor's appointments and received all his immunizations on time. He developed normally. He slept, ate, and played like any other child. I went by what I learned in my parenting class. I made sure to introduce him to the proper stimulation and foods. He was picky and just like any other infant, ate what he liked, and spat out what he did not. I spoiled my son with love. I wanted to make sure that he was a prince; nothing less was acceptable.

Chapter 5

<u>Alone</u>

His developmental progress was on schedule. At six months, he began teething. At seven months, he started crawling. Eleven months old, he was walking, and repeating words like "Mama" and "Nana." Although he was coming along excellent, I was still dealing with the residual effects of childbirth. I displayed symptoms of Post-Partum Depression. Throughout my pregnancy, I gained 75 pounds. Within the first four months of giving birth, I lost 60 pounds. I barely ate and slept. I was irritable and upset for reasons that made no logical sense. I knew something was wrong when I would put my son to sleep, and before falling asleep myself, I began bawling my eyes out with tears.

I was trying my best to cope with the fact that I was not going to have his father to help. No matter what, I made the best of the situation by taking any negative feelings I was enduring and put all that energy towards loving son. Every night we would fall asleep together, and in the morning before getting out of bed, we spend at least 5 minutes playing before we got off the bed. My favorite part of the day was waking up to him. It was an excellent way to begin the day with the sounds of your child's laughter.

Although It was overwhelming at times, I was in a constant lethargic state due to my lack of sleep. It felt as if I would spend days driving on pure adrenaline. I felt like I only had one purpose, and that was to stay focused on the objective of being a responsible parent. After a while, it began to take its toll emotionally. I tried to find constructive outlets to help cope with my feelings.

Another Try

I reached out to friends and family for distractions and to find time for myself. It was around this time that I reconnected with an old friend I met in the military. He was helpful and supportive. He always kept me in good spirits. He came to visit my son and me numerous times and tried his best to comfort me.

I thought that his actions were one of a true friend; it turns out it; they were from a persistent admirer. After a while, I knew he had fallen for me because he kept saying, "I'm in love with you." I guess because I was agitated continuously or going to some emotional breakdown, it took a while for me to acknowledge it. "Although you have a child with someone else, it doesn't matter!" He said. "He abandoned you and gave me the chance to be the man to you that he wouldn't or couldn't." "you right..." I said, reluctantly agreeing. "He's gone" It was right, and to have someone be so brutally honest using such a sincere tone made me despise and love him for it.

He was a good friend throughout my pregnancy and became an even more critical part of my life when he became my confidant. I opened to him about everything. Having a child and being abandoned, the last thing I wanted. I was to steer myself away from the path of such an immense heartbreak occurring again. I valued our friendship and just appreciated the companionship that he offered. His attempt to court was not in vain.

He tried his best by spending time with my child and me. He accompanied us to Doctors' appointments and bought me flowers whenever he sensed that I was getting either upset or frustrated. When we began the relationship, he was everything I could have asked. He was attentive and caring. I was warned and told several times to be careful because It is effortless to get pregnant after your first child. So, I guess it came to no one's surprise that within a couple of months, I became pregnant once again.

Within the first twenty-four hours of finding out, he proposed to me. It was both a confusing and exciting time. He wanted to get married by his birthday, which was three months away. We both decided on a small wedding, no more than fifty people. I could not wait to tell my family the great news. They were confused yet elated that I was finally going to get married. Unfortunately, a week after telling his family, his father passed away.

Alone Again

At the time of his passing, his father was living in Port-au-Prince, Haiti. He owned a house, sold after his death. The profits split amongst his four children. My fiancée decided to use his portion of his inheritance at our wedding. I spoke to him the day he left the country to sign the papers and receive his money. For three days I had not heard from him, it was not like him to go that long without communicating with me. I began to get worried about his safety. I called his phone relentlessly for a week, and I received no reply.

One late night, I received a phone call from his sister, who informed me that he arrived, stating that he was dead and murdered during a robbery attempt. I was utterly devastated by the passing of my son's father. It was worst because his sister did not know of our engagement. It was an uphill battle convincing her that I was pregnant with his child.

She thought I was a delusional Gold digger (at best). His body was in Haiti, where the rest of his family decided to have a funeral. I was informed about the details two weeks after. I thought I was finally going to have the family that I have always longed. It seemed fate had other plans for me because I was left abandoned, again.

The Second Time Around

This time around, I had a child and pregnant with another. My prospects took away from me. Whatever plans I had to be happy, was not meant to be. I could not believe fate could be so cruel. While still mourning, I had to face the future on my own again. It was not hard to accept being alone anymore, and it was just something I had to learn to endure.

Although I spent my pregnancy depressed, I tried my best to stay healthy and composed for my unborn child and the child that was to come. The thought of being a single parent with two kids scared me more than just one. It was downright horrifying. I never wanted that for myself, and especially for my children, I always aspired to have a family. Regardless of what I might have wanted for myself, it was destiny that was the driving force of whatever control I thought I had over my life.

My second pregnancy seemed awful because my emotional state had gotten worse. I was still dealing with Post-partum from the previous pregnancy and hormonal changes from the current. I felt like a wreck. My parents were supportive of the second child as they were for the first, but this time it was different. It did not feel like the happy time it was supposed to be, no. It felt like a burden — not my child, but for me. I had gone through so much. I began to have all these negative thoughts run through my head daily. The negativity subsided a bit to give way to a slither happiness when I found out the baby's sex. I was happy to know that I was going to be giving birth to another boy. Sadly, the feeling did not last for long.

Until the day I gave birth to my son, I was depressed. I did not have a baby shower, and I was not eating as much I did the first time around. I had gained 60 pounds compared to 75 pounds before. I was discouraged because I became a statistic, another single mother. I would have fewer chances of success due to decisions I made of my fruition. Luckily, I had some close friends and family that would try to help. I found comfort in my cousin's best friend. We knew each other for years, and he was close to my family as well. He began to visit frequently.

He was always there when I needed him. Whenever I needed something to eat or even a couch buddy to watch television, he helped me with my first child; therefore, our relationship grew. He became my best friend. I was not interested in anything romantic, and I just wanted someone to talk. I guess I chose to ignore what was visible to everyone else.

At that point, He had fallen for me. It was incredibly bad timing because my due date was arriving, and I was about to give birth to my second baby boy, Christian. During all that was occurring around him, my firstborn son was doing very well. I always made sure to give him the best version of myself. He was learning to speak; we were already effectively communicating his needs. He was being potty trained and knew how to walk and play just like any child his age.

Although he was a picky eater, I made sure that I taught myself how to cook and that I provided for him. Before I knew, the day came, and I gave birth to my second son. The second time was much different from the first. I had done it before and knew what to expect. My Doctor was the same as the previous delivery. She was such an excellent coach, and throughout the process, I could not think of any else I would have delivered my child. It only lasted for four hours, and because I was dilating so fast, she decided that it would be too dangerous to get an Epidural. They were worried that the baby might also be "drugged up" to maneuver out of the birth canal.

I requested local anesthesia, but they were worried that I would not have the energy to push. I would have to undergo a "C" section to deliver the baby. I did not want my child to be drugged and did not want to experience a C section. I went with plan C, and that administered only a small amount of anesthesia to help soothe the pain, and I would take care of the rest (literally). Not only did I push, but when he was out and shoulders, they allowed me to pull him out of me. The Doctor (surprised herself) hands me the scissors to cut the umbilical cord.

After the birth of my second child, I went through a long period of Depression. I was in a constant state of sadness and loneliness. I became withdrawn from the world. I made sure that no matter what way I felt about my life, I would not make my children suffer. I was not feeling like myself, and I would cry incessantly between daily baths and feedings. I would still feel irritable, discouraged, unhappy, tired, and moody. When I did not want to "feel" emotions, I slept as often as I could. I knew I could not continue without seeking professional help. I did and diagnosed with Post-Partum Depression.

My mother and Stepfather were supportive, but I still had to do everything on my own. Despite all the negative things that occurred, I wanted to snap out of it. I tried to wake up from a bad dream that seemed never-ending. I tried my best to think positive thoughts. After a while, I had to learn to be happy. I did not want to let my circumstances deter me from being grateful for giving birth to two healthy boys. I would not let my consequences stop me from being the best mother that I could be.

Chapter 6

<u>New Commitments</u>

Meeting for the First Time

Being the only child afforded me the blessing of being spoiled. Even though I was depressed at times, I was happy that my son would grow up differently. Unlike me, he was going to have someone to grow up with and share secrets and experiences with someone that he would have a bond to for the rest of his life. I had a clear vision of my boys meeting each other and creating a healthy relationship.

He was a relatively small baby. He weighed a little over six and a half pounds when he was permitted to come home. He was exasperated. My mother picked us up and drove us back. He was asleep throughout the whole ride. We arrived at the house people were waiting outside to meet the new addition. Opening the door, everyone was just so surprised that he was so small and fragile. Christian was coming home for the first time faced with mixed reactions from his older sibling.

His older brother took his first glance and was fascinated, curious, and excited. He was encouraged at the sight of another baby and a new companion. The baby was still asleep and was not aware of his surroundings. I did not want to disturb him, so I kept him in the car seat. We brought him in at sat him in the middle of the living room floor, so everyone had a chance to see and quietly interact with him. In the meantime, William ran to his room and grabbed his favorite Teddy Bear. He briskly walked up to his brother and shoved the toy next to him.

Startled and awoken from his rest, the baby began crying. Worried that he was going to be in trouble, he abruptly ran to his room. After calming the baby down, I needed to reassure William that he had not done anything wrong. I explained. "Your baby brother is too small to play with yet."
"I'm sure that he appreciates that you want to share your favorite toy with him."

He looked up at me, smiled, and said: "Really, Mommy??".

I responded, "Yes, my love, he's okay. See for yourself.", "Hold your out arm out so you can hold it to make sure?".

He rapidly held his arms out in anticipation and jumped up and down with excitement.

"You have to be Careful and still when you're holding a baby. Make sure you keep his head up."

He calmed down as I slowly handed him the baby. We smiled and said, "Mommy, he's tiny." I agreed, as we sat and watched him for asleep.

After a couple of weeks of waking up multiple times in the middle of the night and the constant crying, the jovial attitude he once had turned into hatred and jealousy. The lack of sleep because of a newborn, my attention was now being divided. I did not want him to feel left out. When the baby was big enough, I decided to have him help me with daily routines. It was the perfect solution. He liked to help and loved to make his brother smile by making faces. As time went on, it became apparent that William had acclimated his role as an older brother.

With that acceptance came a short period where they bonded with each other. Whenever younger brother began to cry, he would walk up to him and place a kiss on his forehead and pat it. He would get his little brother to calm down. As an only child, it made me happy to see them enjoy being siblings. It is a relationship that I could only envy.

Unfortunately, it was not long before he began to play with his brother less frequently and behaved annoyed when I asked him to help. He began to detest the sound of his brother crying and continuously refused to share his toys with him. Although they were close, it became apparent that William started to change gradually.

Regression

Christian was six months old when William began to display behavior that was unlike him. He was always a playful child. By then, William was healthy, knew how to talk, walk, run, jump, etc. He began to smile less and became silent. They stopped engaging as frequently. He would seclude himself purposely. Unlike children his age who sought attention, he declined it.

He became so withdrawn when addressed; he would always look down or away. My family and I were concerned that he was losing his hearing. I did not want to believe that something could be wrong with him. I decided to test my theory. One day, I went to his room and sat next to him on his bed and decided to converse with him. I called his name for one hour, and to my dismay, he did not look in my direction once. I felt horrible but, at the same time, realize that finding out what was wrong was the most critical information I needed to help him.

The thought of something wrong with my son made me feel devastated. I cried myself to sleep every night. I had the support of my immediate family. The process of getting my son diagnosed would be a hard and long one.

William was always a happy baby, but within that time, he laughed and smiled less. He Played with the most obscure objects hours at the time — objects like strings, rocks, lint, and leaves. I periodically bought him new toys, but they never held his attention as long as the ones he would find.

He was always surrounded by playmates but still preferred to be on his own. He became very picky about what and how he played. He slowly became a perfectionist. He would play with toys that had distinctive colors or shapes. He would align and place toys strategically. He wanted everything in a precise place, or else he felt uneasy. Playdates at the park consisted of him briefly acknowledging other children around him and finding a solitary place. He would go to his favorite sandbox, find something to dig with and go at it for hours. If the other kids attempted to play with him, he would run to me. He became increasingly sensitive to noise. When he felt it was too loud, he would cover his ears.

At the age of 5, his behavior became more erratic. I took him to his Pediatrician and referred to specialists. During the initial portion of the process of his diagnosis, it was also time for him to start school. Feeling an enormous amount of anxiety at the thought of him embarking on such an essential part of his life and still not know what was going on with him. I had no choice but to send him and hope for the best.

First day of school

His first day, I tried to explain what was going to happen and what to expect. I attempted several times, but his short attention span would not allow it. When the day finally came, he woke up early, got dressed, and ate breakfast. It was his first day of Pre-K. We got there fifteen minutes early. I wanted to speak to the teacher. When we arrived, it was deafening because of all the other children.

He walked around with his hands firmly grasped around his ear and reluctant to meet anyone new. When I met his teacher, she introduced herself as Mrs. Gonzalez. While we got acquainted, he decided that he wanted to sit down and look at what he had brought in his new backpack. I explained to her his situation. At the end of the conversation, I gave her my cell phone number to contact me in case of emergencies. She slowly nods and agreed that she would. I kissed my son goodbye and headed home.

While I drove home, I cried. I felt emotionally overwhelmed. I was sad because, like any other parent, I was watching my baby grow up and concerned about his well-fair. Fifteen minutes after dropping him off, I receive a frantic phone call from his teacher, urging me to come back to the school immediately. I rushed to the school as quickly as I could (It was a three-minute drive).

When I arrived, I meant the School's Principal and his teacher. They had a look of alarm on their faces as the teacher proceeded to roll up her sleeve and show me where my son bit her forearm. Her explanation of what happened was inaudible at best. It made no sense. I tried asking William what happened and why he felt the need to bite her. To my dismay, I received no answer. I concluded that whatever the story was, in the end, my son did indeed inflict an injury.

The Principal had to leave for unknown reasons and left her and I commiserating over what occurred.

She then told me, "I'm neither trained nor certified to deal with your son."

"I don't think that I have the ability or knowledge to try to teach him, so you need to take him home!". I replied, "I'm sorry that my son hurt you. It was unfortunate. I agree that I need to take him home, but I don't think that taking such a pessimistic tone will help him or this incident, either."

I took a deep breath and walked away to get my son. I felt nothing short of surprised and a little bit insulted by her atrocious tone. I decided that whatever their solution to the problem. I did not want to deal with it. Immediately I took my child and his belongings and left. I needed time to calm down and reflect on what was best for my son and not my ego. After a couple of days, I received a phone call from the schools' administrative secretary telling me that the incident documented would help with any analysis conducted for his review. I understood that law was required to have my child enrolled in school and have attended when he turned five. I explained that I was already aware of the law and that as a concerned parent, I would NOT have my child under the care of someone who expressed that they were inadequate as a teacher.

She either could not or would not be able to supervise my child correctly. It would have been extremely irresponsible of me to put my child in that position. She was the only teacher left with space; all the other classes were full. I had no choice. I told them that the only course of action I could take at that point is to keep my son home until I found an alternative. The decision to keep him home became the beginning of a battle with the District Public School System, one that would reach our States Governors' Office.

Chapter 7

The Diagnosis

Uphill Battle

I knew that being a parent had its challenges, but I was not mentally or emotionally prepared to deal with it all. I was responsible for two human beings and their growth. As a teenager, I grew to regret some of the decisions that I made for myself (as an adult). Now that I was no longer a child, I could no longer afford the luxury of being selfish. I had to make decisions that were going not just to affect me but others. I could no longer take the risk of reckless or thoughtless choices that could potentially harm my children's welfare and growth.

Having my child stay at home instead of going to school was just the beginning of many difficult decisions that I had to make. A week after informing the school principal, I received a phone call from the Miami Dade County Public School District. Their office received a request to begin a case file for my son. To proceed, I would need to go to their office and formally fill out an application to have it reviewed. My son would need to take the necessary medical exams to assess the cause of his behavior and to determine his "Special" needs.

I agreed that he needed an evaluation, although I refused to acknowledge to bring him to school and be in the presence of someone who would be inadequate to his wellbeing. It was hard enough going through a period of uncertainty relating to my eldest child's health. I would not allow my child to endure neglect due to another's incompetence. I kept my son home for three weeks until the district officials, and I finally came to a compromise.

The decision to comply with the law required me to bring him to school every day and stay with him in class for a minimum of three hours a day. I would have to sit in class with him and made sure that he was well behaved and helped him with classroom assignments, projects, etc. It was a bit challenging to bring his younger sibling to school with me. Required to be assessed by his Pediatrician and referred to specialists for any additional testing.

He was required to get tested for both the school system and for the Social Security Administration to establish his disability Case. He had to undergo several Psychiatric, Neurological, and Physical Evaluations. By the time he began testing, he had utterly stopped communicating. When someone attempted to speak to him, he always looked down and refused eye contact with anyone. It became increasingly tricky talking with him there I had to inform the Doctors that he would have problems comprehending and following instructions.

One after the other, we always had issues. Something that would have been relatively easy seemed somewhat impossible. Could not or would not hold still long enough for the person to perform the exams. He would kick himself out of the chair or attempt to kick the person that was in the way. He just could not communicate with the Doctor or Nurse. After several attempts, they would give up and suggest another Health professional that they felt were better suited to aide me. They felt that their test results would not get effective and conclusive results.

Concluded that he did not have any hearing or visual problems, but some exam results were inconclusive and had to be reviewed by Pediatric Specialists who worked with children with Disabilities. To make sure that he did not have any hereditary conditions, I was required to undergo Blood tests. He had two MRI's (Magnetic Resonance Imaging) taken to determine if he had any brain abnormalities.

After a long process of elimination, his neurologist suggested the possibility that he might have Autism. I had heard of the term before but never knew what it meant. Autism Spectrum Disorder is a neurological and developmental disorder that beings in early childhood and can last throughout a person's life.

It is a condition related to brain development that impacts how a person perceives and socializes with others causing problems in social interaction and communication, including limited and repetitive patterns of behavior. It affects how a person acts and interacts with others, communicates, and learns—called a "Spectrum "disorder because people with ASD can have a wide range of symptoms and diagnoses depending on the severity.

There are five forms of Autism. They include Asperger (a milder form), PDD (Pervasive Developmental Disorder), also called atypical Autism. Childhood Disintegrative Disorder, and Rett's and Kanner's Syndrome. The signs to look for are:

-not respond to their name by twelve months,
- not point at objects to show interest by fourteen months.
Not Play pretend games by eighteen months.
-Avoid Eye contact and want to be alone.
-Having trouble understanding other people's feeling not talking about their feeling
-Have delayed speech and Language Skills
_Echolalia (repeat words or phrases over and over)
-Give unrelated answers to questions
-Get upset by minor changes
-Flap their hands and rock their body, or spin in circles
-Have unusual reactions to the way things sound, smell, taste, or feel.

Acceptance

As much as I did not want to admit it, he displayed ninety-five percent of the symptoms since he was three years old. It was a hard pill to swallow. Without knowing it, I was experiencing a form of grief. 1 out of 48 boys and 1 in 252 girls diagnosed each year, which means Boys are five times more likely to have Autism than girls. Research has also found that the rate of African American children are twice as high as Caucasian children and 1.5 times higher among the Hispanic children than White.

I tried to educate myself on his condition so I could help him and help myself. I knew the statistics of it, but the aspect that interested me the most was the cause. Unfortunately, to my dismay, it has not pinpointed. It may occur as a result of genetic predisposition, environmental or unknown factors. Many people out of "concern" voiced their opinions and determined that I was to blame for my son's condition. A few Simple-minded people thought that because I had my second son so soon that it somehow affected him so negatively that he regressed.

I knew that it was a ridiculous notion, and I would never entertain the thought. I decided to try a more logical approach. I began to think back on my son's medical history and to think of any variables. I could only think of one, his immunizations, and wondered, do Vaccines cause Autism? This question dates to the 1990s. It is called the MMR Hypothesis.

In 1995 a group of British researchers published a study in the Lancet showing that individuals vaccinated with the measles-mumps-rubella vaccine (MMR) were more likely to have some form of bowel disease that those who had not received the MMR. Dr. Andrew Wakefield, M. D. studied a possible link between the vaccine and bowel disease by hypothesizing "that persistent infection with the vaccine virus disrupted the intestinal tissue that in turn led to bowel disease and neuropsychiatric disease (specifically, autism)."

He conducted several additional studies and recommended that the combination MMR vaccine suspended in favor of single-antigen vaccinations given separately over time. Later other scientists worked on similar case studies such as The Thimerosal Hypothesis, a mercury-containing preservative used in some vaccines. In 2001 The FDA was under scrutiny for concerns of Mercury in Vaccines. After investigating it concluded in 2004 that "favored rejecting the hypothesis that mercury in vaccines was associated with neurological disorders. Thimerosal is not in most childhood vaccines. Today, research has shown that there is no evidence between vaccines and Autism.

The whole process of assessment took an entire year and a half. Throughout everything experienced at such a young age, I always managed to stay brave. Unfortunately, after a while, it became clear that it had a lasting effect. Slowly William became traumatized. He feared ANY health professional that wore scrubs — developing a phobia for needles after going through countless "Red" Tapes and tests. Concluded that he's Autistic, He fell on the "Extreme "end of the Spectrum.

After finally discovering what the problem was, part of me was relieved. I no longer had to speculate. Within that, ignorance came fear. I was afraid of what being "Autistic" meant. It said that William would not be "normal" and have the same opportunities that a person without it would have. I felt that people might not understand him and treat him differently. Would he be bullied? Even worse, He' s African American living in the United States. A country that famously and unapologetically murders young men of color without cause.

Chapter 8

<u>Aware</u>

The Realization

As I was learning about his condition, he was getting presumedly worse. He was non-verbal, therefore communicating was extremely difficult. I could not speak to my child. I felt awful. It was an ordeal that I would not wish on my worst enemy. I had to learn to cope with his emotional state when the frustration of not being understood would be the catalyst to his constant outbursts. Occasionally, it would turn physical and need restrained. It was always imperative to keep him calm. Even though we did not understand him, he did follow us. We eventually found a way to communicate effectively.

If he wanted something, I would have him point to the specific object by describing its shape, color, smell, or texture. For example, if he wanted a toy from his toy box, I would ask, "Which toy do u want to play with?" "Do you want the ball or the plane??", "Do you want the Green Roundball or big yellow plane??". Despite the small triumphs, I began to feel sorrow. The more I tried to deny my emotions, the stronger they became.

As time went on, it became apparent that raising him was becoming a mental and physical challenge. Taking him to his routine health checkups became a mental challenge. I looked for health professionals that worked with him children that can be a bit difficult to tend. Referred to a dentist that had "special" methods, and guaranteed results. The day that I took him, I thought nothing of taking him to the specialist.

Arriving early, I had plenty of time to inquire about their methods. After doing x-rays, a preliminary exam, and routine cleaning, William had a cavity and needed to prepare for the procedure during the next visit. We arrived a second time, fully aware, and prepared. They sat him down in a chair that had three straps on each side. The dental assistants tried to calm him but could not. They continued with the procedure, and It was a horrible experience.

He was crying so much and so loud that it drowned the sounds of the other parents and children sitting in the waiting area. The experience was so traumatizing that he urinated on himself throughout the procedure. By the end of the ordeal, He was both soaking wet from the tears and urine. Walking away that day, I had a taste of the mental struggle it would take to be reliable every day. I developed insomnia and found myself continually crying and sad. I was going through Depression. I did not want to go anywhere nor engage with anyone.

I slept as often as I could and was easily irritated. I felt happy and energetic one moment and sad and overwhelmed the next. I expected that many women go through Post- Partum Depression. I would look at my son and break down in tears. I had to try my best many times to not fall apart in public. It was hard to admit that I needed help. I did not want to seem weak or have anyone presume that I was going crazy. Neglecting to acknowledge my faults were not helping me because my sadness and sorrow turned to anxiety. I would cry excessively; then, my heart would start beating rapidly and affect my breathing until it grew more and more difficult to catch my breath. I could no longer stay in such a state. I knew that I could not help my son effectively if I were in the hospital for not taking care of myself.

I finally decided to go to my Doctor and explained everything to her. She referred me to a psychiatrist. The psychiatrist confirmed that I was going through Depression. She prescribed some medications for treating the symptoms and suggested coping mechanisms for dealing with stress. I found that exercising, meditation, and taking time for myself made a tremendous difference with how I dealt with the responsibilities of being a mother. I got myself back on track but learned a valuable lesson about taking care of myself.

The more that I learned about his condition, the more worried I became. I became concerned about his personal and social growth. Whatever selfish aspirations I had delayed. If I were going to make sure that my son was not going to suffer because of his condition, I would have to dedicate everything that I had to his survival.

The issue also grew to be difficult because his behavior became more erratic, and his health began to be affected. One morning, I woke up to my youngest child crying. He was agitated; he had just woken up and hungry for his breakfast. His older brother and I were on a separate bed. I got up and went to feed him when I heard the eldest crying for me. He got up and ran to the kitchen. At that point, he became non-verbal. He stopped talking, and when he did attempt to speak, it was gibberish. I could not understand. It began to frustrate him. After a few attempts to communicate his needs, he just gave up, broke down, and began to cry. He wanted and needed to be understood. The fact that I could not devastate him and me.

He was so upset that he started throwing temper tantrums and tossed anything that he could get his hands on. He kept yelling." No, No, No!!". He kept running around the house, yelling and screaming. I finally caught up to him and managed to hold him. He then dropped himself to the floor and in the fetal position, vividly upset. I attempted to pick him up, but he continued to yell and began trembling.

I let go of him because I thought I was causing it. Instead, he began grinding his teeth and convulsing. His eyes were rolling to the back of his head. His breathing became shallow, and as he was about to fall backward, I caught him. To ensure he would not choke, I quickly placed him on the floor and made sure his airway was clear. It lasted for almost a minute before it stopped. After 5 minutes, he became calm and coherent.

Overwhelmed, I stood over him, wanting to break down and cry. I was scared because it could have concluded another way. He could have died, and I would have felt responsible. I was also angry because he was going through so much at a young age. As a parent, you do not want your children to suffer. That is why we work so hard to protect our children. At that moment, lost on how to fulfill my duty to him. I had to subside all my fears and stay calm for his sake. I took him to the hospital and referred to his Neurologist for a follow-up. Warned that if he were to have a convulsion, he could have a seizure easily. In case of another emergency, Prescribed Valium for attacks lasted longer than 2 minutes and administered rectally.

It was overwhelming (to say the least). To absolve everything that was going on with William. I had to deal with constant employment, social, and emotional issues. Keeping a job grew increasingly hard. It became apparent that I could not have a "laisser Faire" attitude towards childcare. With the youngest child, it was not a problem finding a qualified babysitter, but it was a burden with the eldest. I needed someone who did not have the training, patience, or previous experience with special needs children. They were not qualified.

After my experience, I learned a valuable lesson on being educated and well prepared. Considering the consequences, if I did not do my due diligence, I would consider it is negligent towards my child's basic needs. Although it was tough for me, I know that it must have been hard for him. I decided that I always had to seek the absolute best help for him if he is to have any real chance at a productive and happy life. It was imperative because he was getting worse.

Our family and friends witnessed the subtle changes in his behavior. He was becoming more aggressive when he got upset. He would continuously hurt himself tripping, skipping, or jumping off furniture. He would have horrible gashes and would be bleeding everywhere but seemed not to have any remorse or regret towards being hurt. I could tend to his wounds, and he would get up and do the same thing again. He increasingly became a danger to himself.

I decided to turn all my concerns and fears into the source of my strength. Over time, my tears turned into my determination. My son became my motivation, thinking that he could not lead a healthy life, learn how to drive, go to college, get married, and have children of his own. Everything that I wanted for him seemed so inconsequential compared to what he was experiencing. I could only imagine the world through his eyes. He could not understand what people around him were saying. Constantly feeling lonely and misunderstood, no one comprehending what he was saying and feeling.

Advocate

My son did not have a voice. Figuratively and literally, he was nonverbal. My life dedicated to helping fight for his. I searched to find adequate resources. I joined CARD (Center for Autism and Related Disabilities) at the University of Miami. They "provide support and assistance to optimize the potential of people with Autism and related disabilities. I discovered other organizations such as The Dan Marino foundation whose mission is "empowering individuals with autism and other developmental disabilities through therapies, research, education, and employment in pursuit of a greater quality of life."

Every year it sponsors a special event called "Walk About Autism." This event is a family fun walk and resource expo that brings thousands of individuals together to generate autism awareness, promote understanding, and raise needed funds for the local Autism community. I felt that it was vital for me to gain as much knowledge as possible and recruit as much help as possible.

After my experience with his Pre-K teacher, I realized the importance of having competent and capable people who have the same objective of my son's growth. Everything that he had to endure, I had to make sure that he was getting adequate aid. I needed to be educated on him as well.

We fulfilled all the state's mandated requirements for the Exceptional Students Aide school program and the Social Security Administration for disabilities. The Special needs program recognizes children with learning and social impairments and provides the resources to ensure that students receive adequate services relating to their assessed needs. He was to transfer from his home school to one that could better accommodate his needs. To choose the best program, I could interview a representative from each school.

After discussing the benefit of each school, I decided to go with the one that would help nurture his talents. It would turn out to be the best decision that I could have made for him and one of many to come — from that point on, required to attend an annual IEP (Individualized Educational Plan) meeting with the staff assigned to work with him. The goals include a condition, observable behavior, and mastery criterion.

Benchmarks are mandatory for students with disabilities who take the Florida Alternate Assessment to the Sunshine State standards, annual goals, and criteria based on PEN (priority Educational Needs). It measures the student's strengths, Social and emotional behavior, Independent functioning, and communication.

The team consisted of a staffing specialist, his ESE teacher, Speech-Language Pathologist, Principal, and Vice-Principal. His low cognitive ability required extensive direct instruction to accomplish skills needed for domestic, community, leisure, and vocational activities. The priority was to find an educational setting that provides the proper accommodations, including educational services, specialized instruction, specialized transportation, assistive technology devices, and communication needs.

I was considering the factors before placing him in the least restrictive environment. His frustration and stress, self –esteem and worth, disruption of students in general education classes, distractibility, need for lower pupil-to-teacher ratio, the time required to master educational objectives, social skills causing increased isolation and difficulty completing tasks. It was pertinent that he joins a program that nurtured his talents. His love for music and playing the piano is an essential part of his identity and self-confidence. He needed an opportunity that would allow him to explore and grow as an artist.

The program had a tremendous impact on him, and He attended for his 1st-grade year until his 5th. He had the same primary ESE instructor for three years and attended Speech Therapy sessions twice a week. The team then assigned to him did a phenomenal job of patiently comprehending his tendencies and respecting him as a person. His disability was not an excuse for his limitations. They focused on his independent functioning and less reliance on assistance.

With their help, he was able to learn to speak. At the age of 8, he began to refer to me as "mommy," and at nine, he was finally capable of saying, "I love you." Although his speech still comprised of gibberish, he even attempts to communicate and displays less frustration. If he needs something and is not verbally communicating effectively, he draws a picture diagram of what he desires. Taught to identify his emotions and express them. For example, I will ask, "are you okay?" "How was your day today?" "Are you feeling good or bad, happy or sad?". Assessing his emotional state makes it easier and helps to delegate the response to his behavior.

Chapter 9

<u>Coping</u>

Part of the Psychological assessments required the family health history of his father. Being abandoned by him was hard to deal with, now I needed him. I searched for several months before I was able to locate his sister and mother. I had them relay the message that he needed to be there for his son. After three months, I received a phone call from him asking to meet with me. We agreed to meet at a public park, a five-minute destination that felt like longer.

My son and I arrived before he did. When he came through the park entrance, he parked his car two spaces away. I got out of the vehicle, grabbed my son, and proceeded to wait as he approached us. He took a long look at his son, looked up at me, and said: "Hi, how have you been."

"We're doing just fine," I replied. I was not in the mood for a small banter. Jumped right in headfirst and began to discuss absence in Williams sons' life and his plans to be present AFTER we establish paternity. He impregnated and abandoned me and, at that moment, blatantly insulted me.

It took all my will power not to engage. I had to set my pride aside and think of my son. I agreed to his terms and even offered to pay for the

Paternity test. During the conversation, William had been restless and cranky because he was hungry. I let his father take him to a nearby food store to grab a snack. He bought him a 50-cent bag of chips and a 25 cent individually packaged juice. They walked out of the store happy, William had a smile on his face, and his father also seemed content; therefore, I assumed everything went well.

The next day, on my, to work, I stopped at that store to get some coffee. I ran into my son's aunt and two of her friends. They asked to see my him, seeing no harm in it I agreed. My good intentions went awry when they began laughing at him. "What's so funny?" I asked.

Hi, Sister looked up at me and replied, "Nothing...." She chuckled,
"I won't lie, he looks just like my mom, but I hate to be the one to tell you. He's going around saying that he does not know why I'm asking for help and does not believe that it is his son because he doesn't make sick babies. "

Floored, I could not believe that he would continue to add insult to injury. I tried my best to take it all in with stride, but it was all in vain. It is evident that no matter what, he would try to find a reason not to take responsibility for his son. I decided that he was not worth the fight. He did not deserve to be a part of his life. I would have the burden of submitting all his health evaluation with just half of his family history. His father's side would have to be considered null and void. After that day, we lost contact with him and have not attempted to search for him again.

A Brother's Love

Despite the crushing disappointment with his father, he needed to develop long term and dependent relationships with the rest of his immediate family. I was not blessed to have a sibling, and I was the only child. My youngest son, on the other hand, was lucky. Unfortunately, he did not see it that way. Growing up, the boys were relatively close. Before his older brother began going through changes, they were always together playing and laughing. My youngest was five years old when his older brother started the process of his diagnosis. It was during this time that William separated himself from his little brother, and their relationship changed.

As time went on, he noticed that his brother was a bit different from him. Wanting a playmate in his brother. Instead, he had to deal with the sad truth. At times, his brother would reject him. He would attempt to speak to him as he would look down on the floor. His brother was living in his world. He continuously felt ignored by him and grew resentful.

He found some of his habits odd and did not understand why he would do what he did. He became jealous of the extra care and attention that his older brother was receiving. One thought that the other was gaining a little more attention. I never wanted my children to feel neglect or jealousy. I tried my best to be there for both. I loved cherished and appreciated them. They are the words I want to come to mind when my children think of me.

I had to explain to my youngest that his brother is different in a unique way. He is the same because he has emotions and needs love like anyone else. He sees and reacts to things in his way. Regardless if he does not understand the reasoning behind the actions, he still needs to be respected as a human being. My youngest one could not comprehend why he was "normal," but his brother was not. "What is "normal"? I explained.

"We are all different. We experience and view things differently. No two people think EXACTLY alike. What one person considers healthy might be "Weird "or "Different" to someone else." "It's in the eye of the beholder."
Despite the communication barrier, they eventually found ways to play together and mend their relationship. As they grew older, they cultivated their relationship from what they had in common: hobbies, favorite songs, Television shows, toys, or songs. Finding common ground between them opened the line of communication for them. I did not want him growing up to resent his brother for any reason. I wanted him to love him, not shunned. I knew how that felt.

My Solution was at any time he feels like he is being ignored, mistreated, or have any type of grievance, I encourage him to talk about his feelings. Keeping them bottled up will cause him to grow hate or resent his brother and me. Whatever he is feeling, harmful, or positive, I want him to express himself. I always make sure that I am available to listen and not make him feel bad for any negative feelings. He needed to know that his happiness is just as important.

Without being prompted, he decided that he would help with caring for his older brother. He would help with everything from grooming to dressing him. I praise him often. He needed positive reinforcement for his efforts to understand and cope with the difficulties of having an older brother with the mental capacity of a "Little Brother," the role was reversed.

His Perspective

Having a child with a disability requires diligence and patience. At times it gets overwhelmingly frustrating due to other's lack of knowledge of your child's medical condition. Daily chores that needed taking him out in public were the times it would be on prominent display. He loves to watch television and repeats phrases from his favorite shows. In social settings, he attracts attention, and people stare as we walk around while he makes facial expressions and sporadic hand gestures. Speaking to himself in repetition. He stopped and frequently plugged his ears to silence the world around him.

The stares would consist of confusion and intrigue. As William continued to display this behavior, I began to see it from another perspective, his. No one around me can understand what I am feeling, thinking, or saying. I knew that his condition would not affect his immediate family; our love was unconditional. I was naïve in thinking that it would not change strangers' perceptions towards him. I have brought up with the lesson that it is impolite to stare. I quickly saw that many people were not privy to that lesson.

At times, it was not entirely their fault. Young children bewildered by his behavior would look at him and turn and ask their parents, "What's wrong with him?" or "That kid is acting funny, is he okay?". Several times I found myself explaining his behavior and educating others about his condition. I tried to explain it from his perspective, what it feels like to be him. I found that the best way to tell "what does Autism feel like?" was to refer to the analogy of "The Frayed Wire" (Sealy, Lori." The Aquila Report," 2016).

When you go to your Stereo and turn on the music, with the speaker wires working, the sound becomes apparent. The experience is excellent and pleasant. However, if the speaker wire has a short in it and the sound is not so clear, the connection could be lost. When the cable is in its proper position to allow the frequency to flow, the music heard clearly.

If there is even a small shift, then the wire will produce static and sparks (pain). Despite the music still playing, there is a competing noise that turns the pleasant experience painful. There is a sudden shift, and the simple static turns to immense and agonizing white noise. Harsh sounds that hurt things shift once more, and the wire is in a non-functional position. The connection is gone, and you are in silence. The Stereo itself is still making a melody but trapped inside the machine.

Chapter 10

<u>Perception</u>

Normal

Part of educating others was explaining to others was to tell that he was still a child, just different. The only thing that many considered "Normal" was the way their brains functioned. "Normal" is not a phrase that I like to use because no two people think alike, and everyone has free will and thinks for themselves what constituted as usual. It is a concept that is subjective. Depending on how the person was nurtured growing up, their culture or religion. What is considered "Normal" to one part of the world might be utterly appalling to another society of people opposite their spectrum.

Many people diagnosed with ASD have issues with communication, social, verbal, and motor skills. For example, he cannot brush his teeth nor feed or bath himself because of the lack of motor skills and assistance and supervision. Some children with ASD are self- sufficient, and some are not. No two people with ASD display the same symptoms. Due to their limited ability to communicate, they stay in their "own world" and have limited interactions with others. Therefore, they have difficulty understanding others and developing proper language and functioning skills.

Some children like him deal with uneven language development. Their speech and language skills are not well developed. They may take longer to comprehend what they have learned. They sometimes do not respond to the common language spoken around them. Not even to their names. Some may understand and able to converse. Unfortunately, some have issues knowledge with the speed, tone, and infliction of the language of others their age, which makes interacting difficult.

William's Echolalia (repetitive and rigid language) affects his ability to be social. Some children like him will say things that have no meaning. Due to their verbal skills, they become frustrated and act out inappropriately. Other children find it hard to cope with or understand and choose not to interact with him out of fear.

Sensitivity to Noise

When he is in an environment that becomes too noisy, he will feel uncomfortable and want to leave immediately. Hypersensitive hearing of specific frequencies has sometimes associated with Autism. Many children with ASD suffer from different hearing issues such as Hyperacusis (intolerance for familiar environmental sounds) or Phonophobia (an abnormal and persistent fear of music). Others may have Misophonia (an emotional reaction connected to a trigger that a few people who are emotionally close to the affected person) and Recruitment (hearing loss). Certain sounds and pitches become intolerable and even painful and a trigger for anxiety attacks.

Therefore, to remedy the problem, I bought noise-canceling headphones. It helped regulate his mood and accommodated his needs. We will not go to places that have too many people because they tend to be too noisy. I must be mindful of his condition when I interact with others. If I let my tone and volume get too loud, it becomes a catalyst to his fears, acting irrationally. Playing at school or on the playground was difficult if the environmental conditions (noise level) were not perfect.

Eating Habits

Williams's condition affected several aspects of his life. His eating habits were one of them. He became very picky with what he ate. As a baby, I was strict about serving him the right healthy foods. As he grew, certain foods had to have a feel, smell, look, texture, and temperature. He would continuously eat the same meal until he became tired of it. For example, for breakfast, he would eat cereal and eat A Grilled Cheese sandwich for both Lunch and Dinner. He would have the same meal for three months or more. Until he decided that he wanted to try something else.

He only finds a handful of foods acceptable and never diverts from the menu. Being "picky" makes it difficult to convince him to try something new. When he does manage to eat something that he likes, for example, Burger King Chicken Nuggets, bought from a specific restaurant ordered right out of the fryer because It must be consistent in its texture and touch. He will not eat anything that is overcooked, smells, or looks different than what he expects.

Childhood development is not simple for children with ASD. The ability to transition from one phase to another is a complicated process. Most children generally drink from the bottle from birth to 9 months. Experts have suggested that "prolonged use of the bottle can lead to tooth decay and nutritional deficiencies in young children."

Generally, children transition to the "Sippy" cup phase (a cup that has a detachable lid with a projecting hole), then graduate to finally using a "Regular" or "Big persons" cup. He was extremely slow. He was still using "Sippy cups" until he was twelve years old.

Emotional/Mental State

Keeping a child's mental state healthy is an essential aspect of their growth. When children first enter school, they are taught to identify what they are feeling and coached on how to express them adequately. It can affect a person's actions, relationships, and their overall view of society. In some instances, due to the lack of communication, children with ASD may not be able to articulate their emotions, and parents do not understand what and how to fix problems.

Many of them depend on their actions to display their needs for attention or affection. Their behavior reflects their immediate experiences, and it dictates how they interact. For example, On a school day, if William has a negative experience before his day officially begins, then he will be in a lousy mood and shut down for the rest of the day, making it difficult for others to communicate or aide him.

Others queued his emotions in his environment. Whomever, he felt close to, he would take on their current emotional state. If I am upset about someone or something, he will get angry as well. I am watching a sad movie and start to cry. He sat next to me and began to sob. It was his attempt at understanding me and showing that he cares for others around him. He is very attentive to other people's feelings. He always has a smile on his face and wants to see the people he cares for as happy as he. He lives in "his world," so it is hard for him to fully comprehend some of the negative aspects of life unless they directly affect his day to day routines.

Like any other child, he looks for love and acceptance. When they feel that they do not have a voice or not understood, it can carry negative consequences. The desire sometimes manifests with negative behavior such as outbursts, hitting himself, others, or objects. Shutting down or crying because of sadness or disappointment. Some parents (like myself) endure the physical ramifications of their condition. His behavior sometimes turned violent. He would attempt to hit me to show his disapproval. Once he developed this behavior, I tried different ways to support his emotional state of mind.

I drew pictures of faces expressing mixed emotions. We made sure that he learned and recognized them. Throughout the day, he was tasked to identify what he was feeling good, bad, or indifferent. If he were feeling any negative feelings, I would ask him why he felt that way. I tried to calm him down by rubbing his back or any other triggered points of relaxation. I would change his environment by taking a walk around the neighborhood or a drive to the park. If there was a need for intervention, I had his brother distract him and find something that they both would enjoy. Developing networks of support helps tremendously. Socializing frequently with Friends and Family helps with social skills.

Finding healthy outlets of self –expression is paramount to growth. Encouraging helpful and optimistic thinking and positive reinforcements for their achievements helps to elevate their self -confidence. Some autistic children struggle with necessary motor skills. However, when honing these skills, they may choose music or art. By drawing pictures or playing instruments, it allows them to communicate their thoughts and feelings, opening a window to better understanding the child and their needs. Taking the time to acknowledge, encourage, and nurture their expression forms will help keep them on a stable wavelength.

My son's art displays his perception of the environment, me, his brother, and the rest of his family. It encompasses what he fears, loves, and wants to be. It has always surpassed my expectations. He is as meticulous as he is with everything else. He creates cartoon characters and recreates the scenes from television shows he loves and enjoys. Drawn by memory, He has even crossed over to architecture. He makes 3D designs of houses and buildings from popsicle sticks, paper, and sometimes unconventional materials such as leaves and cotton balls. His condition has not stifled his creativity but expanded to different forms.

His love of music has been apparent since he was a baby. He could repeat a song that he heard after a few times. He played the piano with no formal lessons and practiced every day. He then began to try other instruments to compose. If he did not it then he created, it. He made a small Guitar out of a bowl and eight rubber bands and a drum out of a bucket.

Capacity to Learn

I did not have any expectations with his condition, and I only wanted him to do his best. To my surprise, he performed well in school. He excelled in many subjects, especially math and reading. He can calculate math problems in his head without using paper, a pencil, or a calculator. It took some time, but he eventually knew how to read by the age of 8. Despite having a short attention span. From the third grade on, he has always done well in school.

Grades consisted of A's and B's rarely does he earn a C.

His capacity to learn depends on his interest in the subject. Keeping him on task is difficult. I made sure to devote the time to ensure he completed all his classwork and homework. The goal was he comprehended what he learned and could apply it to everyday life.

It required a lot of patience because it may take several attempts to embrace a lesson. Once he put in the effort, I wanted to give him the reward or acknowledgment that he accomplished his goal. Fortunately, his condition amplifies the importance of nurturing his talents, boosting his confidence, and making his emotional and mental wellbeing a constant priority.

S

"Double-Edged Sword"

Bullying

Parents fear for their children's general safety at school; those who have children with disabilities sometimes experience more stress because there are more variables to their lives that cause concern. They want their children to have the complete experience of growing up and being a student. Accommodations are made according to the child's condition and needs. To ensure the child is in a healthy and productive learning environment.

If a child with Autism is non-verbal, it may be difficult to understand "Stranger Danger" or speaking up if they are being bullied or mistreated by their peers. They do not report it because, generally, they cannot understand when they are targeted. Autistic children make easy targets for school bullies. In recent studies, 46% of autistic children in middle and high school victimized at school compared to just 10% of the general population. (Time Magazine, "Why Autistic Kids make easy targets for school bullies" Szalavits, Maria). September 2012.

Children with Autism who are high function (high intelligence and speak well) are more likely to be bullied than those who suffer from low IQ and unable to speak. They can interact and communicate while sometimes displaying some form of social awkwardness. With disabilities hazier to peers, it makes it harder for them to understand their real plight. Children secluded from the general population and enrolled in Special Education are less likely to encounter it. Many programs implement distancing from the general student population. Since the early 2000s, there have been many campaigns to "End Bullying" in schools across the United States. It has been linked to the cause of many teenage suicide cases.

Studies have shown that schools that create an environment that encourages inclusion from both the students and Adults perform better academically. Unfortunately, because of fear and an ongoing stigma about people with special needs, many generations have no experience with them and do not consider them fully functional human beings. Then the next generation continues the cycle once they have passed on their incomprehension.

A mother who contributed to a survey recounts what her autistic child had to endure. "He had possessions stolen, possessions urinated on, and the one that he found the most traumatic, he was grabbed by another student in the change rooms after the gym and shoved into a shower stall," she explains. They turned the water on him while other people looked and laughed." "He was also bullied by his teacher. If he asked too many questions, she would get irritated and send him out of the class for the duration of the lesson."

Many Children that go through these traumatic events do not receive justice for the crimes committed against them, many racially motivated crimes. In February 2017, a 19-year-old white man named John K. Howard was on trial for putting a coat hanger up the rectum of an autistic black male. They were both in high school at the time of the incident. Called racist insults like "fried chicken," "watermelon," and "Kool-Aid." The parents of the young man reported the bullying, but the school did nothing because the white male came from an "important" family in their community.

After taking legal action to ensure his day in court, The District Judge concluded that the crime was not racially motivated and did not constitute a sex crime. They approved a plea deal for a lesser charge and did not include ANY jail time for his crime. He was sentenced to community service and probation, a clear example of the cruelty and injustices that they face.

In 2018 Being Black in America is a daily struggle for your life. Historically, racism has sown the fabric of its society. The Puritans (Pilgrims) left England because of religious persecution, they came to Plymouth Rock, Massachusetts, with the need to establish dominate, conquer, and colonize other's domain. Using the Doctrine of Discovery provided by law and divine intention, European Christian countries gained power and legal rights over indigenous non-Christian peoples. Various European monarchs and their legal systems developed this principle to benefit their own countries.

Once they set foot on the land and introduced it to the Natives, the outcome was predetermined. The Pokanokets (also called Wampanoags) controlled the area that was settled by the pilgrims. Their leader signed a treaty with them and taught them how to survive and thrive from the land. But after some time, the Pilgrims began asserting their Political jurisdiction, in the name of God and acted as usurpers of the Natives' fundamental rights. Violence abrupted, which led to the genocide of Pequot, 700 Indian men, women, and children massacred at their annual Green Corn Dance. The next day the governor declared a "Thanksgiving Day" in honor of their victory thanking God for the bloody battle they had won. ("Thanksgiving: The True Story by Penny Colman) September 2012.

The settlers set a precedent for the establishment of dominance and control in the new land. They needed to build and expand their colony. Slavery was the most profitable venture at that time. They created the Transatlantic Slave Trade, a trading network between America's, West Africa, Europe, and the Caribbean. Their ships first left European ports carrying copper, cloth, slave beads, guns, and ammunition to West Africa. The cargo bartered for African Slaves that were then transported to America and used to farm Cash crops like cotton and tobacco exported back to Europe.

Slaves were dropped off in the Caribbean islands to cultivate the land and extract their resources like sugar and spices. The country became very wealthy, and it became the primary resource for profit for many years while overlooking the atrocities perpetrated against the slaves that helped build its wealth. In 1760 the Industrial revolution began to change that with the invention of the cotton gin. At the end of 1840, significant advances in the manufacturing process made slaves less of a necessity. While slavery was prevalent in the South, it was abolished in the North. In 1861, unable to agree on the direction of the country by eliminating the institution of slavery, their conflict escalated and began" The American Civil War."

The North won the war, but the generation s after that the South would never forget its defeat and would not let the rest of the country and world forget. In January of 1863, President Abraham Lincoln signed the Emancipation Proclamation, which declared all Men, Women, and Children beaten, mutilated, sodomized, and murdered into servitude were finally free. For years, the South and people who have the same views of racial superiority instead of equality, have made it their goal to have a society that is exclusive instead of inclusive, separate, and not equal.

From the seed of hatred and bigotry, fanatical cults such as the KKK (Ku Klux Klan) arose. A white supremacist hate group whose mission is to oppress people of color. Through legislation, corrupt Civil servants passed laws that promoted extinguishing fundamental human liberties. Deterring voter registration suppressing their constitutional rights. Throughout the years, Segregation in society became acceptable. They were separating African Americans and Caucasians in all facets of society. The term "African American established to enforce separation from the other races legally socially.

Countless men, women, and children of color suffered from injustice. The worst example of this was on August 24, 1955, 14-year-old Emmett Till allegedly flirted with a white woman in Money, Mississippi. After four days of searching, two white men found, tortured, and murdered him. At the trial, the jury of all Caucasian males found them "Not Guilty," and they were set free. At the funeral, his mother decided to have an open casket for the world to see. It was his brutal and unjust murder that galvanized the Civil Rights Movement. In 1964, Congress passed the Civil Rights Act to ensure the Civil Rights of all citizens. Throughout the years, The United States has passed many laws that promote the equality of its citizens. In 2017, the woman that accused Emmett Till (the widow of one of the men involved) confessed that she lied.

On November 22, 2014, Tamir Rice, 12 years old, was gunned down by Ohio two police officers. He joins Michael Brown, a teenager fatally shot by a police officer in Ferguson, Mo. And Trayvon Benjamin Martin, a 17-year-old African American from Miami, Florida, was fatally shot by George Zimmerman, a neighborhood watch volunteer. He felt intimidated by a teenager wearing a hoodie and carrying a can of Arizona Juice cocktail and a bag of skittles. He followed the young man, shot, and killed him.

Placed under arrest for the murder but acquitted under the "Stand Your Ground, "a law passed in 2005 with the help of the NRA (National Rifle Association). It permits a person that feels reasonable threat or bodily injury to "meet force with force, including deadly force" rather than retreat. (billofrightsinstitute.org). My concern is for the person that may feel "threatened" by my son because they do not understand his illness and use "deadly force."

In April 2017, a Florida cop charged with attempted manslaughter in the shooting of an Autistic Man's Unarmed Therapist. While an unarmed caretaker was trying to c down his patient, the officer shot him in the leg. We live in a country where we cannot rely on public civil servants to protect and serve the community. Instead, they terrorize it. I have to black sons who one day will grow up to be black men. (Miami Herald, "Cop shoots caretaker of an autistic man playing in the streets with a toy car," Charles Rabin. July 20, 2016).

Children need to know the status-quo, the fundamental ways their society functions. It is becoming paramount for every parent of color to have "The Talk." Explain to their children, once they leave the comfort of their home, the color of their skin makes them a target for those with malice in their hearts. We must teach them to do all the right things and to make sure that they stay alive.

Staying Hopeful

Saying "I worry a lot" is an understatement. I become devastated at the thought of anything terrible happening to my children, so I try my best to protect them. Many parents must endure the same or worse. I have learned that immersing myself with knowledge and meeting others that experience similar circumstances makes it easier to deal with. Knowing that I am not alone and having the resources has made a significant difference in my son.

Since I have learned of my child's diagnosis, I have also heard of many instances with parents with children who have ASD completely give up and abandon their children. Or parents who do not (or could not) protect their child adequately and become a victim of rape. There are nuances to each situation, some easier to deal with than others, but we are all different therefore analyze and engage towards dilemmas differently. Learning about the consequences of not being cautious motivates me.

I experience a lot of mental and physical stress. To function, I have found that there needs to be a balance. The responsibilities of parents with children who suffer from mental or physical disabilities sometimes surpass those of their counterparts. Staying fit, mentally afloat, and spiritually fulfilled sustains me. I do my best to take time for myself to meditate, take a warm shower, jog, read a book, or even paint. Indulging in my hobbies allows me the opportunity to relax and rejuvenate.

I try to approach a situation prepared to deal with anything that may occur. It requires patience and diligence to maintain. I am the first line of defense for my children, doing as nature intended. There are plenty of resources and guidelines for effective parenting, but no assurances of the outcome.

Chapter 12

Stay Strong

His Future

As he grows older and interacts with others. It is essential to have the foundation set so that he can communicate his feelings effectively. The most important thing I want for my children is that they live Independent, long, productive, happy lives. Many parents with children worry about the care that their children will receive once they are no longer living. As the parent ages, they must weigh the options of long-term care. They may consider leaving the responsibility to a sibling or family member.

They may not want to burden others and decide to place their child in a facility that offers the services that the individual requires. I have had the privilege of meeting many people who have children with Autism or work with them in Speech Therapy, Classroom Instruction, or Behavioral counseling. During the process of writing this book, I took the opportunity to interview a couple of people that helped inspire my journey. The person that I chose both worked with children with disabilities and had a child with Autism.

Mr. A. Bullock was my youngest son's fourth-grade teacher. He was exceptional at engaging with the students and motivating them to nurture their identities and not to follow others. He had a tremendous impact on my son's life. On the day that I decided to thank him for being such a positive influence in my son's life, I brought William with me. As I introduced them, he explained that he had three children, two daughters, and a son. He was also autistic.

I knew that he worked with children with disabilities, but I was not aware that he had one. I was encouraged to find another parent that understood what I endure daily. He said, "My wife and I have two daughters and a son. We love him very much. Even though he is my stepson, I am remarkably close to him; we do everything together. The problem began when he got older, and it became harder to keep him calm. His emotions would trigger erratic behavior that my wife could not physically handle."

I could tell it was not easy for him to explain it without getting emotional. His demeanor softened as he continued, "One of the reasons that I love my wife is because she is resilient and will do anything for her children. The problem became worse when he's erratic behavior started to affect the girls." "It became harder to contain him or help subside his emotions. When he became physically overwhelming to deal with, we decided that it was best to place him in a facility, and that can better help him grow and acclimate."

His face buried in hands adamantly, stating that they did what was best for him.

"We visit at least three times a week, and he loves it. It was hard at first, but he seems to be getting better and likes the environment and the group of people that works with him. It was not an easy decision. We did what was best for everyone."

He finished a small indent smile on his face. He loved and cared for his children and did what was best for his son. Others that work with children with special needs must have an incredible number of patients. It is a calling to work with kids that have immense growth and cognitive issues. They do not do it for the money because a lot do not get adequately paid for the hard work that they do. I commend those who do so with an open heart because they realize the importance of what they are doing.

Final Message

Wanting the best" seems to be the reoccurring theme with all parents that love their children. I want William to have a "regular" life, one that is independent. Driving a car, going to college, having a job, a wife and children, a family of his own. I want him to be happy. I am no different from any parent that lived at any point in time. Of any race or religion in any corner of the earth. A mother's love is the same in ANY language or species.

Any parent that feels overwhelmed or alone in their journey, please know that you are blessed. With a person that can love you like no one else. If you have a child with special needs, make "Loving them" and not "Enduring them" the priority. The decisions that must be faced will not be easy but are worth it. You must Stay strong and do your best; your best is all that you can do.

On this path, I have learned that all I can do is be persistent, Diligent, patient, and loving. Try being patient, nurturing, and caring in all matters. Do not feel shame or sadness but proud to have brought such a unique soul into the world. To always "Lead with Love." Once I am no longer physically on this earth, I want my children always to remember that love transcends life and death. The joy I shared with them will be the love that cradles them forever.